YANKEE
WISDOM
New England Proverbs

YANKEE WISDOM
New England Proverbs

Wolfgang Mieder
Silhouettes by Elayne Sears

The New England Press
Shelburne, Vermont

Library of Congress Catalog Card Number: 89-61223
ISBN 0-933050-73-9

Second printing, October 1991
Third printing, July 1996
Fourth printing, July 2001

For additional copies of this book or for a
catalog of our other titles, please write:

The New England Press
P.O. Box 575
Shelburne, VT 05482

or e-mail: nep@together.net

Visit us on the Web at www.nepress.com

Contents

CONTENTS

Introduction

New England encompasses so many different historical, cultural, geographical, and sociopolitical aspects that it is difficult at times to understand how this relatively small region of the northeastern United States can be looked at as having any unity at all. Considered individually, the six states of Connecticut, Maine, Massachusetts, New Hampshire, Rhode Island, and Vermont have their own distinctive characteristics. The Maine fisherman, for example, certainly is different from the Vermont farmer; the Bostonian executive has different concerns from the Portuguese immigrant to Rhode Island; and the liberal values of residents of Connecticut suburbs seem to clash with the values of the more conservative residents of New Hampshire, whose state slogan is the proverb "Live free or die." The populations of Boston, Providence, and other large cities with universities, cultural centers, and industries appear to conflict with those who live in the quaint villages, farmlands, and woods of the more rural states. In fact, a case could probably be made for dividing New England, if not into six independent entities, then at least into two halves: Maine, New Hampshire, and Vermont would constitute the agrarian and less-populated half, and the more southerly Connecticut, Massachusetts, and Rhode Island would comprise the more densely populated, urban, industrial half with their various ethnic groups. These regional similarities aside, New Englanders have always expressed deep-rooted identity with their individual states. The mere suggestion of combining them into one New England state would be unthinkable and absolutely unacceptable to these independent personalities.

Given such state-to-state distinctiveness, what then ties these six small states together into one New England? Without doubt, it is the common political history they share as the cradle of the United States, which has given rise to the almost mystical image that Americans have of the area as a whole. It was on the coast of Massachusetts that the Pilgrims settled, and it was there that they established the life-style based on Puritan ethics that prevails to this day. Common basic religious beliefs, high moral principles, and austere existences gave rise to a common mentality or character among New Englanders: all value conscience, work, independence, thriftiness, ingenuity, ruggedness, duty, tenacity, simplicity, conservatism, taciturnity, pride, candor, and a particularly dry sense of humor. A common adherence to these traditional New England virtues (and in extreme cases perhaps vices) constitutes the Yankee character, the New England state of mind. Self-reliant and individualistic people carved out a worldview that to this day permeates the nation and helps interconnect millions of people of different ethnic, religious, and social backgrounds.

Much has been said and written about the mind-set and attitudes of New Englanders. Scholarly books have treated their history, culture, geography, society, and politics in much detail. Also well treated have been their manners, customs, and beliefs in this region of rugged seacoasts, large forests, green or white mountains, lakes, rivers, covered bridges, old farms, endless stone walls, white churches, and town halls. In addition to learned treatises, many popular publications capture the New England spirit and mystique, ranging from beautifully illustrated books and magazines to pamphlets and postcards. The region's rich folklore—with its legends, tall tales, folk songs, and weather lore—has long played a significant role in perpetuating the Yankee character and worldview from one generation of New Englanders to the next. Yet up to this point no one has portrayed New Englanders using their wealth of proverbial wisdom, even though the proverbs clearly reflect, at least in part, commonly held attitudes, mores, and experiences of particular areas. To a limited degree proverbs, as concise statements of apparent truths that have currency among people, can be of help in understanding New Englanders even better.

For this purpose over five hundred New England proverbs have been assembled here. Of course New Englanders also frequently use such nationally and internationally known proverbs as "Rome was not built in a day," "Big fish eat little fish," "One hand washes the other," "In wine there is truth," "Man does not live by bread alone," and "A prophet has no honor in his own country." Such standard proverbs often originated in classical or biblical times and were disseminated internationally through translations. The original settlers of New England also quite naturally brought an entire stock of English proverbs with them, many of which remain current throughout the United

States. Examples like "The early bird catches the worm," "Early to bed and early to rise, makes a man healthy, wealthy and wise," "A stitch in time saves nine," and "The proof of the pudding is in the eating" quickly come to mind. Such well-known proverbs, perhaps overused and cliché-like by now, have intentionally been excluded from the present collection. The emphasis here is rather on proverbs that are used primarily in New England.

Some of the proverbs here are without doubt indigenous to New England, such as "Hitch your wagon to a star" (coined by Ralph Waldo Emerson in 1870) and "If you don't like the weather in New England, just wait a minute and it will change." But the origins of other proverbs used in the area, such as "Money is flat and meant to be piled" and "Out of old fields comes new corn," are much less clear. It must also be remembered that as the Puritans moved farther west, they took their proverb lore with them, so that many texts that originated in New England came to be known beyond the New England boundaries, especially in New York, New Jersey, and Pennsylvania. Only painstaking historical research could possibly establish the precise origin of each individual proverb. The complexity of proverbs' origins and dissemination is perhaps best illustrated by the proverb "Good fences make good neighbors." It has existed in this wording only since 1914, when Robert Frost used it in his poem "Mending Walls." Yet it appeared earlier: "A good fence helps to keep peace between neighbors" stems from 1640, and the very similar variant "Good fences preserve good neighborhoods" dates from 1815. But today only Frost's version is current in New England and most of the United States. Summarizing both the landscape of stone walls and the reserved nature of New Englanders, this text can fairly be considered a true New England proverb.

The proverbs contained in this collection were collected both from oral use and from literary writings. Many were recorded during twenty years of listening to verbal communication of New Englanders. Others were found in books and folklore journals on New England in general or on specific states. Of special value were the twenty-five volumes of *Poor Richard's Almanack* (1733–58), published by Benjamin Franklin. These volumes contain many proverbs (some coined by Franklin) and were widely read in early New England for education, moral uplift, and entertainment. Even more influential was Robert B. Thomas's *The Old Farmer's Almanack*, which appeared for the first time in 1792 and is still being issued today, the oldest continuously published yearbook in the United States. Countless readers have benefited from the proverbial advice contained in its nearly two hundred volumes. Another major source of proverbs was the literary works of such New England authors as Edward Taylor, Cotton Mather, Ralph Waldo Emerson, Nathaniel Hawthorne, Henry Wadsworth Longfellow, John Greenleaf Whittier, Oliver Wendell Holmes, Harriet Beecher Stowe, John Godfrey Saxe, Henry David Thoreau, James Russell Lowell, Herman Melville, Emily Dickinson, Louisa May Alcott, Rowland Evans Robinson, Mark Twain, Dorothy Canfield Fisher, and Walter Hard. These authors all used proverbs in their prose and poetry to mirror the regional folk language and wisdom of New England. Their literature helps establish which proverbs were in use in the Northeast in their day.

Ralph Waldo Emerson in particular—the New England preacher, rhetorician, essayist, transcendentalist, philosopher, pragmatist, and humanist—was deeply interested in and intrigued by proverbs. He collected proverbs himself and interspersed them freely in his letters, journals, sermons, lectures, and essays. For Emerson, proverbs are the "language of experience" that "give comfort and encouragement, aid and abetting to daily action." He characterizes them as "rules of good householding," whose "practical wisdom" teaches "worldly prudence." According to Emerson, proverbs are to be understood as "metaphors of the human mind" that express "moral truth" and transmit "their commentary upon all parts of life." In an 1829 sermon, Emerson states summarily that "much practical wisdom passes current in the world in the shape of vulgar [i.e., common] proverbs." The truth of these statements by Emerson is borne out by the proverbs contained in the present collection, for they do in fact comment on all aspects of New England life, including even stereotypical images of New Englanders' independence, ingenuity, thriftiness, and taciturnity. Proverbs contain wisdom regarding all the concerns and tribulations of life. They continue to be employed as comments on human relationships, be they personal, social, or materialistic. The proverbs in the seventeen chapters of this small collection reflect—at least in part—the mind and character of New Englanders, and as such they represent a treasure trove of traditional Yankee folk wisdom.

INGENUITY
AND
COMMON SENSE

Drive the nail that will go.

Use it up, wear it out, make it do,
or do without.

Look at the mark not your arrow.

He who has sense has strength.

The time to pick berries is when
they're ripe.

Don't hunt two hares with one dog.

A mouse can build a home
without timber.

15

Edged tools never wound you when you
are used to them.

When the grain is weedy,
we must reap high.

Hope for the best, and prepare
for the worst.

In a horse trade you've got to know either
the horse or the man.

Reach for the high apples first—you
can get the low ones anytime.

You can't catch the wind in a net.

Hunger will break through a stone wall.

Don't send a boy on a man's errand.

Business neglected is business lost.

Dirt will rub off when it is dry.

Milk the cow which is near.

It's a long stovepipe that has no elbow.

If it ain't broke, don't fix it.

Don't worry about why a black hen lays
a white egg. Get the egg!

An ounce of mother wit is worth
a pound of clergy.

You can't put an old head on
young shoulders.

God sends every bird its food, but He
does not throw it into the nest.

There are more ways to the wood
than one.

A dog is a man's best friend, but a
cow is more help at the table.

If you breed a partridge, you will
get a partridge.

Drive your business, or it will drive you.

It takes a crank to start the wheel.

CHARACTER
— AND —
REPUTATION

There's as much odds in folks as there
is in anybody.

As one tends the fence, he also
tends the farm.

The rough shell may have a good kernel.

Judge a man by his works.

Some people aren't fit to root
with a pig.

Habits are hard to break.

Danger makes men bold.

"Can't" is a tramp that sits by the
roadside and begs.

An empty house is better than
a bad tenant.

A man between two lawyers is like a fish
between two cats.

If you haven't enough to do, start cleaning
your own backyard.

You can't expect anything from a pig
but a grunt.

A hint is about as good as a kick
to some people.

An old wound may be healed, but not
an ill name.

Cowards are most often in danger.

Tongue double brings trouble.

Reputation is dearer than life.

Boston folks are full of notions.

He that has no teeth cannot crack nuts.

19

When all men say you are an ass,
it is time to bray.

Patience is a flower that grows not
in every garden.

Scheming seldom has success.

He who has no shame, has no conscience.

A New England man
is a go-to-meeting animal.

If your head is wax, don't walk
in the sun.

Some women aren't all maple sugar.

The man with no business is
the busiest man.

Great necessities call out
great virtues.

A good name is better than bread.

Boston is a state of mind.

Reputation is a jewel whose loss
cannot be repaired.

Put a bag of coffee in the mouth of hell,
and a Yankee will be sure to go after it.

Glass, china, and reputation are easily
cracked and never well mended.

INDEPENDENCE
—— AND ——
PERSEVERANCE

The toughest skin will hold out
the longest.

Everyone has a right to a tune on
his own fiddle.

The world is your cow, but you have to
do the milking.

It is better to be a horse than a cart.

Love your neighbor, yet don't pull
down your hedge.

There is no hanging a man for
his thoughts.

Independence is better than riches.

Step by step the ladder is climbed.

Every man must be either the hammer
or the anvil.

The more free, the more welcome.

There's no use keeping a dog
and barking yourself.

Live free or die.

An ounce of decision is worth a
pound of doubt.

Touch my property, touch my life.

Let every tub stand on its own bottom.

Paddle your own canoe.

Sooner or later perseverance achieves.

A bird in a cage will fly away.

Better death than a slave's life.

Let every man drink from his own bottle.

When a task is once begun, never leave it
until it is done.

Confidence is a plant of slow growth.

Every sow has to bury her own nose
in the swill.

Grain by grain the hen fills her belly.

A squealing pig gets fed.

If you would have your business done,
go; if not, send.

Let every man skin his own skunks.

Fractures well cured make us more strong.

The squeaking hinge gets the most oil.

A man may kiss his cow.

If you want to get to the top of
the hill, you must go up it.

THRIFTINESS
— AND —
POVERTY

Economy is the easy chair of old age.

Despair never pays any debts.

He that speaks ill of the mare
will buy her.

At a good bargain pause awhile.

When poverty comes in at the door,
love flies out at the window.

Foolish spending makes poor ending.

Nothing should be bought that can be
made or done without.

Beware of too great a bargain.

Creditors have better memories
than debtors.

No purchase, no pay.

Keep your shop, and your shop will
keep you.

Willful waste makes woeful want.

Poverty and peace is better than plenty
with contention.

Don't start economizing when you are
down to the last dollar.

Light purse, heavy heart.

Hunger never saw bad bread.

There are two sides to a bargain.

The more play, the less dimes.

An empty purse puts wrinkles in the face.

Many lose more in a day than others
gain in a year.

He who buys what he does not need will
sometimes need what he cannot buy.

Borrowing makes sorrowing.

Economy is the poor man's bank.

A small home is better than
a large mortgage.

Poverty wants some things, luxury many
things, avarice all things.

Take care of the dimes, and the dollars
will take care of themselves.

Debt is the worst kind of poverty.

Discount is good pay.

Necessity never made a good bargain.

There's no disgrace in poverty, but it's
damned inconvenient.

The borrower is a slave to the lender.

Out of debt is out of danger.

An empty purse is a poor
traveling companion.

LOOKS
AND
APPEARANCES

You can't tell whether an egg is good
by looking at its shell.

Beauty does not make the pot boil.

Seeing is believing, but touching
is the truth.

If you wish to see Old England, you must
go to New England.

Virtue is but skin-deep.

You can't judge a man by his overcoat.

Looks are nothing—behavior is all.

It isn't always the bell cow that gives
the most milk.

There are a great many asses
without long ears.

Money and good manners make
the gentleman.

Wrinkles and patches don't show on
a trotting horse.

Virtue may not always make a face
handsome, but vice will certainly
make it ugly.

Men and melons are hard to know.

Fine fruit will have flies about it.

Dimple outside, devil inside.

You can't judge a horse by its harness.

Appearances aren't everything.

The grass always looks greener in
the other fellow's yard.

All are not saints that go to church.

You can't always tell by the looks of
a toad how far he can jump.

Fine feathers don't always
make fine birds.

Looks are one thing, and facts
are another.

You can never tell the depth of the well
from the length of the handle
on the pump.

Finery and poverty go together.

Handsome apples are sometimes sour.

Dogs show their teeth when they
dare not bite.

You can't judge a cow by her looks.

Beauty is a very fine thing, but you
can't live on it.

HE-HAW

IGNORANCE
— AND —
WISDOM

A closed mouth makes a wise head.

Experience is the mother of wisdom.

There's less pain to learn in youth than
to be ignorant in age.

Knowledge is the best insurance.

Guts can sometimes do more than brains.

Wise men think twice before
they act once.

Experience keeps a dear school, yet fools
will learn in no other.

Answer a fool according to his folly.

He sees best who sees the consequences.

Many complain of their memory,
few of their judgment.

An ignorant consent is no consent.

Adversity makes a man wise.

A full belly makes a dull brain.

Little minds run in the same ditch.

Durable trees make roots first.

Anger and pride are both unwise.

The fear of God
is the beginning of wisdom.

An ounce of experience is worth
a pound of theory.

Where sense is wanting, everything
is wanting.

Knowledge and timber shouldn't be much
used until they are seasoned.

Learning has no enemy but ignorance.

Age listens to the voice of experience.

The more riches, the less wisdom.

A wise man knows his own ignorance,
a fool thinks he knows everything.

When the well is dry, we know the
worth of water.

An eagle's mind never fits
a raven's feather.

Experience is the best rule to walk by.

There are many witty men whose brains
can't fill their bellies.

SILENCE
—AND—
SPEECH

Talking will never build a stone wall
or pay taxes.

Words may show a man's wit, but
actions his meaning.

Turn your tongue seven times
before speaking.

Talk is cheap, but it takes money
to buy whiskey.

Well-timed silence has more eloquence
than speech.

Well done is better than well said.

Speak little, do much.

Be swift to hear and slow to speak.

Deeds are fruits, words are but leaves.

What you don't say won't ever hurt you.

A kind word is never lost.

A New Englander answers one question
with another.

Never speak loudly to one another unless
the house is on fire.

Great talkers, little doers.

Better slip with foot than tongue.

Words are but wind, but seeing
is believing.

Be silent, or speak something
worth hearing.

Hear before you blame.

Three can keep a secret if two of
them are dead.

A good word now is worth ten
on a headstone.

He that speaks much is much mistaken.

Talk less and say more.

Good words cost nothing.

If you have to whisper it, better
not say it.

A man of words and not deeds is like
a garden full of weeds.

If you can't say good things of others,
keep your mouth shut.

Let not your tongue cut your throat.

Talk is cheap; it doesn't cost anything
but breath.

Many words won't fill a bushel.

A talking man is no better than
a barking dog.

Half-witted people speak much
and say little.

Silence is prudence.

What is said can't be unsaid.

One deed is worth a thousand speeches.

MEN
— AND —
WOMEN

You have to hoe a row of corn with
a man to know him.

A barn, a fence, and a woman always
need mending.

Love is meat and drink, and a
blanket to boot.

Keep your eyes wide open before marriage,
half shut afterward.

Choose a wife rather by your ear
than your eye.

In love and war no time should be lost.

Marriage halves one's rights and
doubles one's duties.

Men aren't worth the salt of
women's tears.

Love is too dainty a food to
live upon alone.

Bachelors are but half of a
pair of scissors.

It is a poor house that can't
support one lady.

Never take a wife till you have a house
to put her in.

A deaf husband and a blind wife are
always a happy couple.

Matrimony is not a word but a sentence.

A man in passion rides a mad horse.

An old maid doesn't know anything but
what she imagines.

A house without woman and firelight is like
a body without soul or sprite [spirit].

Kissing a girl because she is willing is like
scratching a place that doesn't itch.

A reformed rake makes the best husband.

Silks and satins put out
the kitchen fire.

The best furniture in a house is
a virtuous woman.

It is well to be off with the old love
before you are on with the new.

An old man marrying a young girl is like
buying a book for someone else to read.

It's a lonesome washing when there's not
a man's shirt in it.

A good wife and health is a man's
best wealth.

Faults are thicker where love is thin.

A warm-back husband and a cold-foot
wife should easily lead a compatible life.

There's no help for misfortune but
to marry again.

OPPOSITES
AND
CONTRADICTIONS

It's better to be neat and tidy than to be
tight and needy.

One eyewitness is better than
ten hearsays.

It is one thing in the mill, but another
in the sack.

An egg today is better than
a hen tomorrow.

Delights dwell as well in the humble
cottage as in the most splendid palace.

A young man idle and an old man needy.

Hope is a good breakfast but
a bad supper.

If the landlord lives, the tenant starves.

Though the devil is up early, God is
up before him.

Age gives good advice when it is no
longer able to give a bad example.

Cream is thicker than water.

The littler folks be, the bigger
they talk.

Out of old fields comes new corn.

A lie stands on one leg, truth on two.

Great gains cover many losses.

The old affect more by counsel than
the young by action.

Plant the crab-tree where you will,
it will never bear pippins.

If passion drives, let reason
hold the reins.

Virtue can never cling to vice.

He who runs in youth may lie
down in age.

Health is sweet, though the
pill be bitter.

He who feels the benefit should
feel the burden.

If you believe all you hear, you can
eat all you see.

A young twig is easier twisted than
an old tree.

A good cow may have a bad calf.

One today is worth two tomorrows.

Though you ride, remember the horse
goes on foot.

Buds will be roses, and kittens, cats.

Young people don't know what age is, and
old people forget what youth was.

A tinker makes two flaws in mending one.

Give a pig when it grunts and a child
when it cries, and you will have a fine
pig and a bad child.

A small seed sometimes produces
a large tree.

An apple pie without cheese is like a kiss
without a squeeze.

WORK
AND
LAZINESS

The hardest work is to do nothing.

A lazy traveler makes a long journey.

Diligence is the mother of good luck.

An idle man is the devil's play fellow.

Wishing isn't doing.

Laziness travels so slowly that poverty
soon overtakes him.

It's a bad workman that loses his tools.

He that rises late must trot all day.

The more you do, the more you may and
the less you're thanked for it.

People may get more tired by standing
still than by going on.

There are lazy minds as well
as lazy bodies.

Trouble springs from idleness,
and toil from ease.

What is worth doing is worth doing well.

The sleepy fox catches no chickens.

Lazy folks take the most pains.

It is impossible to help those who will
not help themselves.

Those who do little expect the most.

He that neglects to weed will surely
come to need.

Hard work never hurt anybody.

They must hunger in frost that will not
work in heat.

Lazy folks work best when the sun
is in the west.

There will be sleeping enough
in the grave.

Promising is one thing, doing is
quite another.

The quickest way to do many things is
to do one thing at a time.

Plow deep while sluggards sleep, and
you will have corn to sell and to keep.

Idleness is the greatest waste of time.

The lazy dog leans to the wall to bark.

He that does nothing is poorer than he
that has nothing.

A work ill done must be done twice.

A lazy carpenter fights with his tools.

He that observes the wind and the rain
shall not reap.

PRUDENCE
AND
ADVICE

An ounce of prudence is worth
a pound of wit.

A traveler should never laugh till he
gets to the end.

Give neither salt nor counsel until
asked for it.

The early robin looks for worms behind
the early plow.

Don't put your hand in a dog's mouth.

It doesn't pay to fight a skunk,
because if you win, you lose.

There's a slippery step at every
man's door.

Half a loaf is better than no bread.

A little neglect may breed
great mischief.

Cut the leather only where
the shoe pinches.

Better late than never, but better
never late.

A grain of prevention is worth
a ton of remedy.

Don't cut down the tree that
gives you shade.

It is too late to lock the barn door after
the horse is stolen.

Avoidance is better than repentance.

There's no harm in asking.

Prudence looks before as well as behind.

When in doubt, do without.

Advice that isn't paid for
isn't any good.

Stretch your arm no longer than your
sleeve will reach.

Anything worth having is worth
fighting for.

Keep straight, and you'll never get into
trouble or grow round-shouldered.

Take care of the minutes, and the hours
will take care of themselves.

Neglect mending a small fault, and it
will soon be a great one.

A good example is the best sermon.

It is better to prevent an evil than
to attend it.

Honesty pays large dividends.

Do not whistle until you're out
of the woods.

Fortune may fail us, but a prudent
conduct never will.

If you must kick, kick toward the goal.

The deer that goes too often to the lick
meets the hunter at last.

Look before, or you'll find
yourself behind.

Hope well and have well.

A grain of caution is worth a pound
of medicine.

Live while you live, and then die and be
done with it.

Don't throw away the bucket until you
know if the new one holds water.

A crooked road won't get you far.

FRIENDS
AND
ENEMIES

Old shoes and old friends are best.

You have to summer and winter together
before you know each other.

Quarrelsome dogs come limping home

No roof can cover two families.

The surest way to make enemies is to
have too many friends.

There's nothing to be gained by
airing dirty linen.

Cursed cows have short horns.

Strike, but conceal the hand.

Friendship can't stand on one leg long.

The ivy destroys the oak.

Speak well of your friends, of your
enemies say nothing.

Mud thrown is ground lost.

Mistrust is the mother of safety.

Too many friends spoil the dinner.

A quarrelsome man has no
good neighbors.

If you can't bite, never show
your teeth.

Politics make strange bedfellows.

Short visits make long friends.

It makes a difference whose ox is gored.

Two of a trade can never agree.

They that are out will pout.

Love your neighbor as yourself—
but no more.

A friend nearby is better than
a brother far off.

A wise enemy is better than
a foolish friend.

Equals make the best friends.

Good fences make good neighbors.

There is no friendship in trade.

The absent person is always at fault.

Those who in quarrels interpose, must
often wipe a bloody nose.

Better a certain enemy than
a doubtful friend.

He that drinks his cider alone, let him
catch his horse alone.

PROBLEMS
AND
FRUSTRATIONS

One dead fly spoils much good ointment.

A cord stretched too much may break.

Don't swallow the cow and worry
with the tail.

It is easier to build two chimneys than
to keep one in fuel.

There's always plenty of help when
it's not wanted.

Too much oil extinguishes the light.

The last ounce breaks the camel's back.

You can't mow hay where the grass
doesn't grow.

Everybody lays his load on
the willing horse.

The mill cannot grind with the water
that is past.

You got to boil a lot of sap to get
to the maple sugar.

Nothing is done while anything remains
to be done.

The more you stir a rotten egg, the
more it stinks.

A good arrow cannot be made of
a sow's tail.

You can shear a sheep many times, but
you can skin him only once.

Sins and debts are always more than we
take them to be.

An empty sack can't stand.

You can't get wool off a frog.

You can't make a crooked stick
lay straight.

The tongue is ever turning to
the aching tooth.

You can't keep trouble from coming,
but you don't have to give it a chair
to sit on.

Toes that are tender will be
stepped upon.

Half the world does not know how the
other half lives.

Three removes [changes of residence]
are as bad as a fire.

He that spits against the wind spits
in his own face.

In fleeing from the water, do not run
into the fire.

Wine has drowned more men
than the sea.

You can't sell the cow and have
the milk too.

Wishes can't fill a sack.

If you can get over a dog's head,
you can get over his tail.

Other people's eggs have two yolks.

MONEY
AND
WEALTH

Make money honestly if you can,
but make money.

The want of a thing makes the
worth of it.

As the wages are, such is the work.

Vice rules where gold reigns.

Today rich, tomorrow a beggar.

If you would know the value of money,
go and try to borrow some.

He that has a trade has an estate.

Women and wine, game and deceit, make
the wealth small and the wants great.

Great spenders are bad lenders.

Money once gone never returns.

Secrecy is the soul of business.

Prosperity discovers vice, adversity virtue.

Nothing but money is sweeter
than honey.

He that will increase in riches,
must not hoe corn in silk breeches.

Many have by far too much,
but nobody enough.

Money makes the mare go—but not
the nightmare.

If you don't do any more than you are
paid for, you won't get paid for any more
than you do.

Sell not virtue to purchase wealth,
nor liberty to purchase power.

No salary without service.

Not to oversee workmen is to leave
one's purse open.

Dirty hands make clean money.

Nobody will seek riches in a
beggar's cottage.

Lend money to an enemy and you will
gain him, to a friend and you
will lose him.

If you would be wealthy, think of saving
more than getting.

Happiness does not consist
in riches alone.

Put not your trust in money, but your
money in trust.

Banks have no hearts.

Money is flat and meant to be piled.

Wealth and content are not
always bedfellows.

CHANCE
AND
FATE

Many a fair flower springs out
of a dunghill.

Time and chance happen to all men.

You'll catch your death just as sure
as you live.

Today up, tomorrow down.

Opportunity is a precious companion.

It's easy to see but hard to foresee.

Your wooden overcoat [casket] won't
have any pockets.

Lost time is never found again.

As Boston goes, so goes New England.

Great occasions make great men.

Broken eggs can never be mended.

Hitch your wagon to a star.

An apple never falls far from the tree.

What happens once may happen again.

Every wind doesn't blow down the corn.

There is small choice in rotten apples.

Small circumstances produce
great events.

When you buy the land, you buy the
stones; when you buy the meat, you
buy the bones.

Leaves have their time to fall.

One must risk to win.

Two shots never go in the same place.

Old men must die, as well as
old principles.

Since you are not sure of a minute,
throw not away an hour.

There never was a pitcher that
wouldn't spill.

The stoutest heart must fail at last.

Little causes produce great effects.

He that waits upon fortune is never
sure of a dinner.

Opportunities are everything
in love and war.

Even a clock that doesn't run is right
twice a day.

Dunghills rise and castles fall.

There are two sure things—
death and taxes.

SAILING
AND
FISHING

Don't wait for your ship to come in.
Row out and get it!

A sailor has no more business with
a horse than a fish has with a balloon.

There are as good fish in the sea as
ever were caught.

The winds and waves are always on the
side of the ablest navigator.

Little boats must keep near shore.

The highest tides produce
the lowest ebbs.

He that would catch fish must
venture his bait.

Good sailors are tried in a storm.

Once a captain always a captain.

Hoist your sail when the wind is fair.

The tide may turn.

Leave not the harbor in a gale.

When the fish is caught, the net
is laid aside.

As the wind blows, you must set your sail.

The ship in harbor is safe.

Those who come up with a flowing tide
will descend with the ebb.

The waves do not rise but when
the wind blows.

That fish will soon be caught that
nibbles at every bait.

The law was not made for the captain.

A small leak will sink a great ship.

Oysters are not good in months
without an "R."

Little ponds never hold big fish.

What the ebb takes out, the flood
brings in.

Where all have become masters, nobody
is left to throw the water out
of the longboat.

Any port in a storm.

Don't make your sail too big
for the ballast.

Two small lobsters make a big one.

Every wind is ill to a broken ship.

Vessels large may venture more,
but little boats should keep near shore.

Fish follow the bait.

When one is hungry, frescoed walls
can't take the place of codfish balls.

In a calm sea every man is a pilot.

The more whales, the less fish.

Time and tide wait for no man.

Cut your sail according to your cloth.

You must have a ship at sea in order to
burn two candles at once.

Vows made in storms are forgotten
in calms.

Small fish are better than an empty dish.

It is hard for an empty sail to
stand upright.

WEATHER
— AND —
SEASONS

If you don't like the weather in
New England, just wait a minute and
it will change.

A cold day or two or a little ice does
not make winter.

If cows lie down before noon,
it will rain soon.

A swarm of bees in May
is worth a load of hay.

Clear moon, frost soon.

A February spring is worth nothing.

A sunshiny shower
won't last half an hour.

Evening red and morning gray—
sure sign of a fair day.

When the frog goes up the mountain
hoppin', then the rain comes down the
mountain droppin'.

A mackerel sky won't leave
the ground dry.

It won't be warm till the snow gets off
the mountain, and the snow won't get off
the mountain till it gets warm.

Some are weatherwise,
some are otherwise.

Town Meeting is time to put
in the potatoes.

Button to the chin till May be in.

We have two seasons: winter and
Fourth of July.

Between twelve and two
you can tell what the day will do.

70

A winter's calm is as bad as
a summer's storm.

Take off your flannels before the first
of May, and you'll have a doctor's
bill to pay.

A clear, bright sky of fleckless blue
will breed a storm in a day or two.

Fog on the hills,
more water for the mills.

A late snowstorm is a poor
man's fertilizer.

It takes more than one robin to
make a summer.

Wet May makes short corn and long hay,
dry May makes long corn and short hay.

If the rooster crows when he goes to bed,
he will get up with a wet head.

Sap runs best after a sharp frost.

March rains serve only to fill the ditches.

Sun at seven, rain at eleven.

Showers are most frequent at the turn
of the tide.

Evening red and morning gray,
will send the traveler on his way;
but evening gray and morning red,
will heap rain upon his head.

Only Yankees and fools predict
the weather.

A high wind prevents frost.

A fine day is not a weather-breeder,
but a fine day.

A cold wet May
fills the barn full of hay.

Frost year, fruit year.

When the dew is on the grass,
rain will never come to pass.

In New England we have nine months of
winter and three months of damned
poor sledding.